published in the united states by kaleidoscope kids llc

visit us at www.readkaleidoscope.com

kaleidoscope, *kids bibles reimagined*

library of congress cataloging-in-publication data is available upon request
ISBNs
paperback: 9781922405449
eBook: 9781922405999

WELCOME TO KALEIDOSCOPE

First of all, thank you for picking up a copy of Kaleidoscope! We are glad to have you. In the following pages, you'll experience the Bible in a whole new way.

Kaleidoscope was borne from the need to provide a retelling of the Bible for elementary-aged children that is between a "little kid" Bible and an adult translation. In a way, we are the happy medium.

At Kaleidoscope, we are producing single volumes for every book of the Bible. They are designed to read like chapter books, so you'll turn pages and look forward with anticipation to the next volume.

But don't let the fact that we are focused on kids deter you if you are a "big kid!" Good children's books are almost always as good for adults as they are for kids.

Get excited! In the pages that follow, you'll see God's wonderful good news. Our prayer is that his kindness, gentleness, and love will melt our hearts and make us more like Jesus.

As a mom, I longed for a kid's Bible that would keep our children engaged while offering a faithful account of the stories in Scripture. Kaleidoscope is entertaining, responsible, and gospel driven! Good News: The Story of Acts helped our entire family better understand God's great plan to rescue his people to himself through his son, Jesus.

-Hunter Beless
Founder and Executive Director of Journeywomen

If you've ever wondered how the Bible fits together as one, big, beautiful story, then Kaleidoscope is for you. By setting each book of the Bible in the context of the whole story, we're better able to see that God is on a glorious mission, from Genesis to Revelation, to rescue his children from sin and death and dwell with them forever. But this great rescue isn't just for us to read about—we're invited to play a part! Through this series, your kids will better understand God, his Word, and his purposes for them.

-Courtney Doctor
Coordinator of Women's Initiatives, The Gospel Coalition, Author of *From Garden to Glory: A Bible Study on the Bible's Story* and *Steadfast; A Devotional Bible Study on the Book of James*

In over 20 years of Children's Ministry, this is one of the most inspiring tools I have seen to help kids (and their parents) experience the Bible in a creative and powerful way!

-Jason Houser
Seeds Family Worship Leader
Author of *Dedicated: Training Children to Trust & Follow Jesus*

If we are going to be faithful in making disciples of the next generation, the church desperately needs resources like Kaleidoscope where children of all ages can begin to understand the gospel story of the Bible as it is woven through every page. I can't recommend this resource enough!

-Jeff Norris
Senior Pastor, Perimeter Church

As a parent, I want my children to love God's word. I want them to desire to read it for themselves. This retelling of the book of Acts is an excellent steppingstone for children to read and learn the big picture of what God has done in and through his church. It reads like the adventure that it is, for nothing can stop our mighty God from spreading his church!"

-Christina Fox
Writer, speaker, and author of several books, including: *A Heart Set Free*, *Idols of a Mother's Heart*, and *Sufficient Hope: Gospel Meditations and Prayers for Moms*

A beautiful, illustrative idea to help children engage with the Bible.

-Bryan Ye-Chung
Co-Founder of Alabaster Co

Finally, I found it! Because I'm a pastor and a New Testament scholar, I have preached and studied the book of Acts many times. But I have never found a book that made me think, "I wish the children I know could read this"—until now!

-Dr. Jimmy Agan
Senior Pastor, Intown Community Church. Author of *The Imitation of Christ in the Gospel of Luke: Growing in Christlike Love for God and Neighbor*

Kaleidoscope is a wonderful way to share God's praiseworthy deeds with the children in our midst. They will delight to discover God's love for them!

-Dr. Donald C. Guthrie
Professor of Educational Ministries
Trinity Evangelical Divinity School

Ten years ago, it was my privilege to hire Chris Ammen right out of seminary. Here's why: He was a young man who possessed a firm, soul-absorbing confidence in the power of the gospel and a great love for kids and their parents...You hold in your hand a tool that will unleash the "unhindered gospel" on the hearts of your kids, and there really is nothing more important than that.

-Dick Cain
Senior Pastor
Rainbow City Presbyterian

Kaleidoscope helps to bridge the gap between theology and readability for young readers. And I, for one, could not be more excited for resources, like Kaleidoscope, to help give my own children the gospel as they grow.

-Jamie Lynn Dorr
@jamielynndoor

Kaleidoscope fills the need our young readers have - to understand the Bible's own big, beautiful story and take it in as their own.

-William Strickland
President, Mission One

What a perfect way to start the series with a book that is rich in church history that is so often forgotten in children's bibles. I can't wait to recount Paul's journey from beginning to end with my own children.

-Korrie Johnson
@goodbookmom, goodbookmom.com

When our children were young and unable to make sense of the big words in the "big" Bible, we were always on the lookout for resources to help them understand the live-saving, life-giving message of Scripture. How I wish we would have had Kaleidoscope!

-Dr. Mike Honeycutt
Senior Pastor
Westminster Presbyterian Church (Rock Hill, SC)

CREATORS

Chris Ammen is the founder of Kaleidoscope and a Children's Pastor in Tuscaloosa, AL. He has a BA and M.Ed. in Elementary Education as well as an M.Div. from Covenant Seminary. When not writing, Chris loves spending time with his wife, Sarah, and their four awesome kiddos!

Maggie is a graduate of Creative Circus in Atlanta where she studied graphic design. When not illustrating, she enjoys her cats, reading, baking, and all things cozy. You can see more of Maggie's work at www.maggiesnead.com.

BACKERS

This first volume of Kaleidoscope is special because it would not have been possible without the support of a community of people who believed in the vision.

Chris: A big thank you goes out to my superstar wife, Sarah, and our four wonderful children: Jake, Caleb, Kate, and Charlotte. I pray this book helps you see Jesus. He loved your dad and gave him new life. He can do the same for you.

Maggie: I'm so thankful for my home church of Trinity in Tuscaloosa and the lifelong relationships that led to this opportunity. Thank you to my illustration teacher, Colleen, for getting me started and Thomas and Henry, my ginger kitties, who sat with me through each illustration.

We are also grateful for friends and family who backed Kaleidoscope through our Kickstarter campaign. The following people supported us in an extraordinary way.

Dan and Ashley Ammen, Mike and Peggy Ammen, Colleen Basler, Dick and Scottie Cain, Sarah and Jake Cain, Michael and Lisa Coop, Allie and John Crew, Tyler and Rose Eads, Neal and Leslie Ellis, Alex and Turner Fain, Diana and Craig Frazier, Ivey and Laurie Beth Gilmore, James Gnan, Jason and Tricia Gray, Nathan and Amanda Hancock, Steven Hebert, Eric and Katherine Heslop, Ken and Kathy Ingraham, Josh and Elizabeth Johnson, Kyle Kasten, David and Liz Kindred, Japheth and Monica Light, Gary and Robin Lake, Grant and Fernanda Luiken, Liz Moore, Rob and Shara Moore, Matt and Katie Pavlick, Carla Peacock, Arthur and Madelyn Pruet, Rockcastle Labs, Alison Ross, Lauren Sheppard, Justin and Amy Smith, Zach and Chelsey Smith, Chuck and Lisa Snead, Matt and Sara Beth Spearing, Stewart and Mary Cannon Swain, Andrew and Kristin Townsley, Doug and Sherrie Tucker, Andy and Erin Turner, Wade and Tut Wilson, & Aubrey and Laura Way

TABLE OF CONTENTS

INTRODUCTION

My grandmother was one of the first female pilots in the United States. I never knew her during her flying days, but I do remember seeing photos and hearing stories of the bravery it took for her to pursue what was then a job only for men. Because of her, I know somewhere deep within me lies the courage to do hard things.

Learning about our family history connects us with the past; men and women who have gone before us and faced the joys and sorrows of this life. Some did great things and others failed miserably! Either way, we can learn from them and gain wisdom.

If it is important to learn about our grandparents, how much more vital it is to learn about our spiritual family! In Acts, we meet people like Peter and Paul. Believe it or not, we are related to them! We are spiritual brothers and sisters. We share the same father in God.

We'll meet lots of other people in Acts, but the most important person of all is God. Stephen and Barnabas were brave, but only because the Holy Spirit was alive inside of them. The book of Acts is not mainly about you, or even about James and Aquila. It is about God and what he has done through his son Jesus to change the entire course of human history.

Let's set the stage for Acts. The author is Luke. He also wrote the book of Luke. Together, Acts and Luke form a two-part series of sorts. Most people think Luke wrote Acts sometime around AD 65-70 with the purpose of telling the story of the early church.

At the end of Luke's gospel, Jesus told his disciples (a name for those who followed Jesus) that they had become his "witnesses." That means they had seen Jesus. They saw his life, his death, and his resurrection. Now their job was to go and tell more people about him. In many ways, Acts is where the disciples live out this call.

In Acts, we get the first examples of what has become the church we know today. The Holy Spirit came to the disciples and they responded by starting communities of believers all over the world. These communities were known as churches, and God filled them with people he would call to be Christians. The church became the way God fulfills many of his promises and shows his kindness to his people.

If this is your first time ever reading about the Bible, welcome! We are so glad to have you along for the journey. If you know it well, explore and discover more of God's good news in the pages that follow.

Let's begin...

MAPS

In Acts, you'll meet people like Paul, Silas, and Barnabas who traveled throughout the known world, telling people about Jesus. These maps here and throughout the book are a fun way to trace their travels.

Acts 9

Acts 13-14

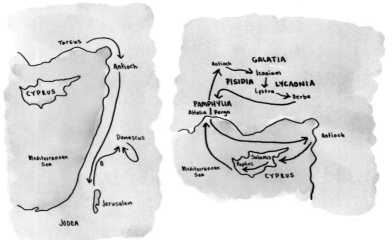

Acts 15-18

Acts 19-21

Acts 27-28

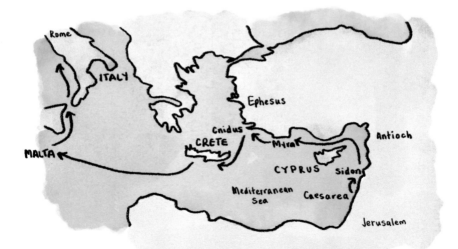

GOOD NEWS ON FIRE!

ACTS 1-2

Have you ever seen fiery tongues fall from the sky?

You haven't? Never?

Believe it or not, it's happened. People saw it, and they lived to tell the tale.

But let's back up for just a minute. You see, before the fiery tongues showed up, God's people had been through a lot! For thousands of years, they waited for Jesus to come. But when he arrived, he was nothing like what they had pictured.

They wanted Jesus to take away the sadness and evil around them all at once. But Jesus wasn't like that. His kingdom was, and still is, one of compassion and kindness. Jesus said his kingdom is like a seed. A mighty oak tree will eventually grow from a tiny seed, but it takes a while. It doesn't happen all at once.

And now, at the young age of 33, Jesus had died. What!? The hero of the story, God's own son, dead?

You got it.

Jesus came and lived the life God says we should: perfect and blameless. He died the death we deserve for our sin (the selfish things we do that break God's heart). He gave his life so we could have life. What a beautiful gift!

Three days after Jesus died, he rose from the grave. Jesus had defeated death! Now he wanted to spend time with his disciples before he went to be with his Father in heaven.

"When will the world be our perfect home again?" the disciples questioned Jesus.

"Now is not the time, and I can't tell you when it will be," Jesus answered. "Only my Father knows."

Their faces fell, worried, wondering what life would be like now that Jesus was leaving.

"Now your job is to tell the world my story, the good news." He spoke in a voice so warm they couldn't help but listen. "Go to Jerusalem, then to Judea and Samaria, and then to the ends of the earth."

But the disciples questioned Jesus, "The world is such a big, big place and there are not many of us. How are we supposed to do that?"

"The Holy Spirit will come. He will give you all the power you'll need."

But the disciples wanted instructions. They wanted a step-by-step plan for how to carry out God's plan to rescue the world.

But a plan would never help them with what they needed most...to learn to trust that the very same God who made the oceans and trees, the God who led Joshua, and who defeated huge armies with tiny ragtag militias was the God who was still with them now.

Just then, a cloud came and lifted Jesus into heaven. Two men in white robes appeared to reassure the disciples, "Jesus will come again; only next time he will bring heaven back with him."

Until then, the disciples had a job to do. Jesus promised them a helper and it wouldn't take him long to arrive.

Only a few days later, wild wind unlike anything the disciples had ever seen swirled down from the sky like a tornado. Tongues of fire filled a room full of people. But this was an unusual fire. No one was hurt. In a bizarre twist, it seemed to give life to God's people...like that burning bush and Moses (remember that?).

As if this was not strange enough, people began to speak different languages and yet everyone could still understand one another. God was making the good news for every language! All of this reminded them of a story their grandparents used to tell them.

In the story, which dates back many, many years, God's people tried to build a tower to get to heaven. When God saw his people trying to make their own way to him, he destroyed it and confused them with all new languages so they couldn't understand one another.

But now, God was making their hearts come alive. Instead of them building their own way to God, he was coming down to them. In place of confusion, he was bringing people together so they could tell the world about him.

In the midst of the fire and commotion, Peter spoke to the crowd, "This is what God promised. What David longed to see is now happening! Repent of your sins and be baptized. This is what you were made for!"

That day in Jerusalem, the crowd of 120 swelled to over 3,000 believers. But this was only the beginning! God was just getting started with his great rescue plan.

A PORCH AND A PRISON (PART 1)

ACTS 3-4

If you want to see a crowd go wild, you should heal someone. Do a miracle. That's what the disciples did.

One day Peter and John were going to the temple to pray. On their way, they stopped at a place called Solomon's Porch. Sitting right outside was a man who'd never walked even one step in his entire life.

All Peter had to say was, "In the name of Jesus, get up and walk!" In the snap of a finger, the man jumped to his feet!

Not only did he walk, but he leapt up and ran around like he was 8 years old again!

Now, the place where this man was healed was not a big town. Everyone for miles around knew him. News spread, and people flocked from all over to hear Peter speak about the miracle. If the good news could heal this man, they wanted to hear more!

"I did not heal this man," Peter began, "It was Jesus. The scriptures you teach in the synagogue told us Jesus would come to bring life to the world. Abraham, Isaac, Jacob, and Moses all announced his coming, but when you met Jesus you hated him and killed him. You deserve nothing but death."

The crowd looked around, knowing they were guilty. A still, eerie hush fell over Solomon's Porch.

"But I tell you, God's good news is much better than you can imagine! Repent, confess your sin, and God will forgive you. God wants to show you kindness and refresh you like a cool, gentle stream in a desert. He wants to bring life to your heart just like he did for this man's legs."

The book of Acts is full of stories of people from all walks of life. Some loved the good news, while others hated it.

Peter was still speaking when some men from the "hated it" group came. They arrested Peter and John and threw them in prison.   .

What was happening? Was the greatest healing this town had ever seen ending with our friends going to jail? Was the good news actually bad news?

The following day, Peter spoke to the men at the jail. "The same God who raised Jesus from the dead also raised this man to his feet. This is the same Jesus you rejected. But by pushing him away, you ran from what your heart needed most. Only Jesus can save you and rescue you from your sin."

Peter spoke like one who really had been with Jesus. Something special radiated off him. The whole town picked up on the excitement. Quickly, the captors realized that punishment was not an option because Peter and John had become the most famous people in town.

After removing their chains, the captors ordered Peter and John to never speak of Jesus again.

This would not be the last time the disciples met people who did not like what they were doing. But the Holy Spirit gave God's people strength and courage to handle each challenge he sent their way.

The "hated it" group would often think they were punishing the disciples. But their plans usually backfired. More times than not, they were only helping the gospel spread!

One man was healed, two disciples went to jail, but over 5,000 people believed in Jesus and were saved that day. The good news could not be stopped.

Or could it?

ANANIAS & SAPPHIRA

ACTS 5

One way the good news changed people is that they stopped hogging all of their belongings. When believers saw someone in need, they were more than willing to give away what they had to help. People were changed forever when they saw how generous God was to them. After all, he had given them his one and only son!

Even so, sin and evil were alive and well. Some people still behaved in the most selfish ways.

A husband and wife, Ananias and Sapphira, had more than they needed. They owned some land and decided to sell it. All of the money, they said, would go to their church for those who needed it. But they lied and kept some of the money for themselves. Ananias and Sapphira tried to hide their dishonesty from their friends, but they couldn't hide it from God.

When Peter discovered this, he grew furious. He called to Ananias, "Why have you lied like this? This is an evil deed Satan put in your heart!"

Before Ananias could even respond, he collapsed to the ground and died right at that very moment!

Three hours later, Peter saw Sapphira and asked her the same question, "What happened to the money? You have lied to God as well!"

Just like her husband, she dropped dead right in front of Peter.

Their friends were shocked. What was God doing? Were the good times coming to an end?

Let's pause for a moment.

You see, some stories in the Bible are easy to understand, while others might leave you confused and maybe even a bit sad. This is one of the most difficult stories in all the Bible. It's heartbreaking and could make you wonder how God could do such a thing. These are good thoughts! You are not wrong for having them.

One thing we must know is that God's wisdom is far greater than ours. He is worthy of our trust, even when things don't seem to make sense. One day we will meet God and get to ask him all our questions. Until then, we can trust him, even when we don't have all the answers.

While not everything about this story is clear, one thing makes sense...

How could the church grow in health with believers who love their money more than God?

Jesus told his disciples, "Do not store up for yourselves treasures on earth. Things on earth get destroyed and stolen. Instead, store up treasures in heaven because your treasure has control over your heart."

Greediness shows us what has real power over our hearts. It has no place next to the generosity of the good news.

A PORCH AND A PRISON (PART 2)

ACTS 5:12-42

God's people were still in shock over the loss of their two friends. The truth of God's good news is wonderful for those who trust and obey Jesus. But the gospel is dangerous for those who don't.

Peter knew more than ever how much people needed to hear and see God's rescue plan.

The disciples went back to Solomon's Porch every day. The sick were healed if Peter's shadow barely touched them. God healed people's bodies of all sorts of ailments. Very often their hearts were healed too as they sensed the kindness of God. People needed this time of refreshment after the tragedy of Ananias and Sapphira!

But things would not stay this delightful for long.

Can you guess what happened next?

If you thought that Peter would be carted off to prison again, you are 100% correct!

But you don't think some measly little prison bars could stop the good news now, do you? Not a chance!

As Peter sat in his prison cell, an angel appeared. Before he could blink, the prison gates were opened. Peter walked right out!

The angel left him with these words: "Go back to the temple and tell the people the words of life!"

The next morning, the high priest and all his big, important men, who hated the good news, came looking for Peter. The gates were shut, the locks were firmly in place, but Peter was nowhere to be found! Their hearts pounded and their bodies filled with fear. Where was Peter?

They searched high and low and around every corner. Eventually, the big, important men found Peter, and he was doing the very thing they told him to never do again.

"We told you to stop all this talk about Jesus!" they shouted.

"We must obey God, not man," Peter replied. "The Jesus you killed wants to save us from death. We must tell people about him."

The big, important men did not like what they heard. These same men nailed Jesus to a cross. Now, they were ready to take Peter's life as well.

But before they could make their first move, one of the leaders, named Gamaliel, stood up and hollered, "STOP! Let's not act without thinking."

Was God working through Gamaliel?

Gamaliel continued, "We have seen things like this before. People come with a new message about God, but they end up destroying themselves, and we don't even have to lift a finger. Let's leave Peter alone. We won't be able to stop him if God really sent him. If his message is made up, like the others, he will fade away. Besides, I don't want to be found guilty of killing God's messenger. Do you?"

Low and behold, the men listened and set Peter and his friends free with *just* a scolding and beating.

God has spoken through all sorts of people and things throughout history: donkeys, prophets, bushes, water, and even fire. In the synagogue that day, he spoke through a man who didn't even believe in Jesus! God will use any means necessary to save the world.

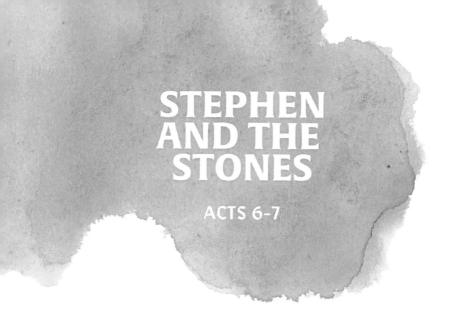

STEPHEN AND THE STONES

ACTS 6-7

Have you ever met someone so brave that you could never, ever forget them for the rest of your life? Stephen was that kind of man.

The church was growing at lightning speed as the good news of Jesus spread. Peter and the disciples had more people to care for than they were able to. What a fantastic problem to have! To help, the disciples called for others to lend a hand.

Stephen was one of the seven men the disciples asked. These men were called "deacons." But Peter, or Stephen for that matter, had no clue what God was about to do!

Almost immediately, in addition to helping the needy, Stephen began teaching the good news and performing miracles. He told people that God sent his only son to free them from living in fear. Jesus lived the perfect life we could never live and took our punishment for all of our law-breaking, sinful ways. We are now free to love God and our neighbors without the fear of rejection.

Strangely though, a group of people called the "Freedmen" didn't like all this talk of freedom. They thought God loved them because they obeyed long lists of rules. But they only fooled themselves. There is nothing we can do to earn God's love. It's a free gift!

Staring at Stephen, they shouted, "Nonsense! We've lived our whole lives following the rules Moses gave us. Who are you to speak against him and change everything? Jesus came saying these same things! Don't you remember what we did to him?"

Even in the face of these angry men, Stephen was not scared. God was with him, and he knew it. God was so close, in fact, that his face even shone like an angel.

Just as they did to Jesus, these men brought others who spoke lies about Stephen. They told awful stories about what he had supposedly done.

"Are these things true?" the leader of the Freedmen asked Stephen.

Instead of taking the easy way out by saying, "No," Stephen used this chance to give a bold and courageous answer.

"Remember Abraham? God told him the good news would go to all the world! Remember Isaac, Jacob, and Joseph? God kept his promises and provided for each of them. Remember Moses? God protected him and his people. Remember Aaron? God showed him how to worship the one true God. Remember Joshua? God used him to lead Israel. Remember Solomon? He built a place to worship God. From the very beginning of time, God's story has been unfolding. Don't you see that this story is still appearing right before your very eyes? Abraham, Moses, and all the others were pointing to Jesus. But when God sent Jesus you did not believe him, and you killed the son of God."

The men's faces drew down into fierce scowls. They ground their teeth in anger as they heard Stephen speak. It was as if their ears were all stopped up with goop, and their eyes were blind. They could not hear or see the good news of Jesus.

But Stephen could see clearly. He gazed upward and saw Jesus comforting him.

Just then, a young man named Saul (more to come on him later), along with a crowd of cowardly naysayers, dragged Stephen outside the city where nobody would see them.

They tore Stephen's clothes off and threw stones at him, one after another, until he lay lifeless. Stephen was dead.

How could this happen? How could Stephen, bold and courageous, die for trying to save people's lives? Before Jesus went to heaven, he told his disciples, "Just as the world did not like me, they will not like you either." In fact, this type of pain and suffering was a part of how God planned to bring his kingdom into the world!

This may seem like a strange plan indeed, but it was full of wisdom and power. God's good news was on the move.

Throughout the Bible, the message God's people hear over and over is that life comes from death. It is very different from the wisdom of the world. The good news tells us that while death is sad, it is not the end. Sometimes it is just the beginning. It's the pattern of following Jesus, who died to give us life.

MAGIC &
MONEY

ACTS 8

After Stephen died, life changed for the followers of Jesus.

The big, important men, who hated the good news, treated anyone who believed in Jesus in the most horrible ways. They took people from their homes, away from their families and children, and threw them in jail in the middle of the night just for believing that Jesus was the son of God!

Life became so miserable that many followers of Jesus couldn't stay in Jerusalem anymore. Believers had to find new places to live as they were driven from their homes. How sad this must have been! In an instant, familiar places and faces were taken away.

Leaving Jerusalem behind, believers traveled to areas such as Judea and Samaria.

Wait just a second!

Judea and Samaria? Didn't Jesus say that the believer's job was to tell people about him in Jerusalem, *Judea*, and *Samaria*? God was turning what seemed like bad news into good news. It seemed as though God had planned it all along!

As soon as he arrived in Samaria, one of Jesus' followers, named Philip, began to tell people the good news. The Samaritans were amazed as he performed signs and wonders. People who spent their whole lives unable to move any part of their bodies hopped right up and danced around like nothing was ever wrong.

One day, Philip met a man named Simon. He was a magician of sorts, although he didn't pull rabbits out of hats or make playing cards appear out of his shirt sleeve! Instead, he claimed to have healing and spiritual powers. But Simon didn't follow Jesus. He made people pay him instead of praising God for these blessings.

If Philip told Simon the good news, would he turn from his ways and trust Jesus?

Amazingly, he did!

When Simon heard about the Holy Spirit, he immediately wanted to be filled with Him, just like the other disciples. But Simon was so confused from a lifetime of people paying him for spiritual gifts that he offered to give Philip money for the Holy Spirit.

"Pay? You cannot pay any amount of money for the free gift of God!" Philip retorted. "You just want the Holy Spirit so you can do magic and make more money. Repent and ask for God's forgiveness."

Simon was sorry and asked God to forgive him.

Simon's story reminds us that even after we trust Jesus, some of our old habits and ways of doing things stick with us. Very often, we have to say, "I'm sorry, God. Please keep changing me."

A little while later, an angel came to Philip and told him, "Go to the south. I have something important for you to do."

To the south? There was nothing but an old, dusty desert down there. But Philip trusted God and obeyed.

While Philip was there, he met a man from Ethiopia. This man helped the queen of his country handle all her money. He was a very important man, indeed.

From a distance, Philip noticed the Ethiopian was reading a book. As Philip drew near, he saw that it was not just any book. It was the Bible. The man was reading from the Old Testament in the book of Isaiah.

"He was like a sheep being led to the slaughter. He couldn't say a word. He was blamed for all sorts of things he did not do and was killed for the wrong things others had done."

Looking up at Philip, the man asked, "Who is this passage talking about?"

The man was reading the words, but his heart didn't understand the meaning. He wanted a rescuer, but didn't know that Jesus had come to do just that!

Philip began to explain that the passage was talking about Jesus. As Philip talked with the Ethiopian, his heart was filled with joy at this chance to share the good news.

Philip talked some more while, out of the corner of his eye, the Ethiopian spotted a pool of water. He asked Philip, "Can I be baptized?"

"Of course!" Philip replied as they ran down to the water and celebrated God's work together.

Then the strangest thing happened. The Spirit of God snatched Philip up and took him away! The two men would never see one another again, but they would always share Jesus and this chance meeting that brought joy to them both.

The good news was on the move. It was spreading to the ends of the earth! The Spirit was living, active, and leading people like Philip to just the right spot at just the right time to tell just the right people the good news!

GOOD NEWS SAVES

ACTS 9

SAUL. Just his name would have sent shivers up and down your spine. Saul was a despicable man who went around killing people who loved Jesus. In fact, he was one of the men responsible for killing Stephen.

Even though Saul knew the Bible better than almost anyone else, he did not believe the good news about Jesus. He would soon find out, though, that he was very wrong.

One day, Saul left his home in Tarsus, traveled through Jerusalem (where he was a part of Stephen's death), and was on his way to Damascus. He had a murderous plan in his heart to hurt even more Christians.

All of a sudden, an extraordinary light from heaven flashed upon him. In a split second, he fell to the ground.

He heard a thundering voice booming as if from heaven, saying, "Saul, why are you hurting me?"

"Who are you?" Saul nervously answered back.

"I am Jesus," the voice answered. "Do you know that you are hurting me by hurting the people who follow me? Pick yourself up and go to the city of Damascus. There, I will tell you what to do."

Saul stood up and shuddered. He tried to look around, but he saw nothing. He was blind! Something like fish scales covered his eyes. The men traveling with him were astonished. They had to lead Saul by the hand, like a child, into Damascus.

This evil man, who was once so strong and mighty, couldn't do anything for himself. For three whole days, Saul could not see. But in many ways, it was like he was seeing for the first time.

About that time, God was speaking to another man. His name was Ananias. He loved God.

"I want you to go and see Saul," God said.

"Not a chance!" Ananias replied, remembering all the horrible things Saul did to his friends.

God insisted, "As strange as it may sound, Saul is going to tell the whole world about my good news."

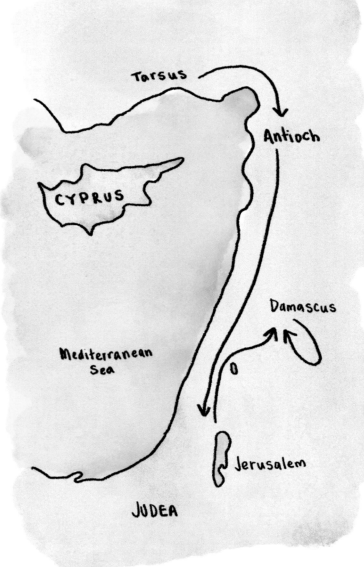

Saul's travels leading
up to and during Acts 9

Ananias trusted and obeyed God. He went to Saul, sat next to him, and prayed. Suddenly, Saul could see again! But he saw the world differently. He didn't want to hurt people anymore. He loved Jesus, and he loved people. This man, who once thought he was big and mighty, changed his name from Saul to Paul, which means small and humble.

Ananias learned that God was telling the world the good news through unexpected people, just like he always had!

Abraham and Sarah laughed when God promised them a child in their old age. It surprised everyone that God used a little shepherd boy named David to do the work of a warrior. People were stunned when a baby born in a feeding trough grew to be the savior of the world.

Now, this. Who would have seen this coming? A murderer was God's chosen person to spread the life-giving good news to millions. This plan was too wonderful for anyone except our God!

PETER AND THE PUZZLING VISION

ACTS 10

A puzzle piece is, well, *puzzling*. That is, until you find the piece it fits with! Shortly after Saul became a believer, God gave two of his followers pieces of the same puzzle. The only problem is that they lived 40 miles apart and had never even met before.

One of those men was Cornelius in Caesarea. He was a wise man who loved God and lived generously. An angel came and asked him to send friends to Joppa to find Peter and bring him back to Caesarea. Of course, Cornelius had no idea who Peter was or what business he had coming to Caesarea. His "piece of the puzzle" did not make much sense. But he trusted that God had a plan.

Meanwhile, Peter was in Joppa when God gave him the other piece of the puzzle. He was up on a rooftop praying when his stomach began rumbling. He was hungry! But before he could eat, he fell into a trance.

God gave him a strange, confusing vision. He saw the heavens open. Something like a sheet, full of all kinds of animals and reptiles and birds, was being let down to earth.

Suddenly a voice spoke, "Peter, you are hungry. Kill any of these animals to eat."

"I can't do that," Peter replied. He remembered that the law of Moses told him to not eat any animal that had been declared "unclean" by God.

The voice answered, "Because of Jesus, all things are clean."

Peter was perplexed. What did all of this mean? The vision, the animals, the sheet, the voice; it was all so confusing! But maybe Peter was puzzled because he only had one piece of the puzzle!

Just then, Cornelius's men arrived from Caesarea looking for Peter. At that very moment the Holy Spirit spoke to Peter, telling him that there were men looking for him. This could not have been a coincidence. God was behind the scenes doing something marvelous!

Peter obeyed the Spirit, followed the men, and two days later arrived at Cornelius's house to quite a large crowd.

"Why have you brought me here?" Peter asked while looking at Cornelius for the first time.

Cornelius explained, "Four days ago I was praying. God appeared and asked me to send for you. We are eager to learn about all that God has taught you."

This was a special moment! In fact, the future of the whole world was about to change. You see, Peter was Jewish and could trace his family's history back to Abraham. But Cornelius was a Gentile, which meant he could not.

People made up fake rules that said Jews and Gentiles were not allowed to be together. They said God loved the Jews and not the Gentiles.

But these "rules" were silly and harmful because God never made those rules. In fact, the good news is so good because it's for the whole world. It doesn't matter where you're from, the color of your skin, or what language you speak. Jesus is for everyone who trusts in him.

The pieces of the puzzle were coming together. The vision God gave Peter was to show him that just as all animals were good to eat, there is no difference in how God feels about Jews and Gentiles. Jesus died for the sins of the whole world, not just one group of people.

Cornelius's puzzle piece seemed to fit right next to Peter's. Why did the angel tell Cornelius to send for Peter? The answer was now clear. God was preparing Peter to tell the Gentiles the good news.

Peter began to share with the crowd, "From now on, anyone who trusts that God sent his only son, Jesus, to rescue the world is in God's family. It doesn't matter where you're from, who your parents are, or what you look like. The whole Bible talked about Jesus, and he has now come to the world. Believe in him, ask for forgiveness, and you will be saved!"

After Peter shared, the Holy Spirit came down upon the Gentiles just like it had on the Jews at the beginning of Acts. Peter baptized the new believers to welcome them into the new family of God.

You would think people would rejoice that the family of God was growing. Normally, you'd be right....

GOOD NEWS FOR GENTILES

ACTS 11

Peter was on top of the world! God did the unthinkable. Gentiles were a part of the family of God. It wouldn't be long, however, before it would seem like everything was crashing down. Peter was on his way to Jerusalem. But news of his time with the Gentiles beat him there.

Some of the Jewish leaders in Jerusalem were not happy. They began to question Peter, "You spent time with the Gentiles!? You know you are not allowed to do that! What were you thinking?"

Peter explained to them the wonderful vision he had right before he met Cornelius. "God showed me that there was nothing to keep the Gentiles from hearing the good news. In fact, the gospel will spread to the ends of the earth just like a sheet covering the whole world! Everything is clean because the spotless lamb of God, Jesus, died for the sins of the world."

The Jews were startled by Peter's vision. Had God really told Peter that the Gentiles were a part of God's family too?

Peter continued, "If you had been there, you would have been just as amazed as me. When I shared the good news with Cornelius, the Holy Spirit fell on the Gentiles just like it did on us Jews. God has done a miracle. Who am I to stand in God's way?"

It was so quiet that you could have heard a feather fall to the ground. Surely, they were about to take Peter to prison again, right?

Wrong! The Jews celebrated and glorified God, saying, "The good news is so good. It is for the Gentiles too!"

Around this same time, another group of Jews, in the city of Antioch, shared the good news with their Gentile neighbors.

As more people in Antioch heard about Jesus, a man named Barnabas emerged as a leader in the city. He went looking for Paul, the man formerly known as Saul, who had recently become a believer. He thought they could be great partners to spread the gospel together.

He was right! For a whole year, Barnabas and Paul worked together in Antioch. They saw God rescue people from all sorts of backgrounds and nationalities. In Antioch, one of the greatest churches in history was built. In fact, it was there people began to call Jesus's followers "Christians."

Some time later, messengers came from Jerusalem to Antioch. One of them, named Agabus, told Paul and Barnabas that soon there would not be enough food for the Christians in Judea.

After seeing how generous God was to them when he gave his only son, the church in Antioch gave everything they could to help their brothers and sisters.

Remember, Jesus said that all who come to Him will never hunger, and whoever believes in him will never thirst. He satisfies us in ways nothing else can. Our hearts melt when we hear that God gave his one and only child to make us his children! This good news built a church in Antioch that became known around the world for their generosity and kindness to others.

The gospel changed people everywhere it went. It started in Jerusalem. Now it had spread to Judea, Samaria, and to the ends of the earth in places like Antioch. It was just as Jesus said it would be.

HEROD THE EVIL KING

ACTS 12

It was not long before Herod, the king of Judea, heard about all the new followers of Jesus. He was not happy! Herod thought of himself as being important and powerful. But fame was not enough for Herod. He was jealous and wanted people to follow him and nobody else. Any talk of people following Jesus was not welcome!

His resentment toward Christians caused him to do many horrible things. In his anger, Herod killed John's brother, James, with a sword and arrested Peter.

But even as Herod tried to weaken and destroy the church, the believers were strengthened. In homes all over Judea, followers of Jesus came together to pray for Peter.

When Peter arrived at the prison, the guards bound his arms and legs with chains and made him sleep between two soldiers. They must have heard about his history as an escape artist. But just like before, an angel came to Peter in the middle of the night. Peter awoke as the angel said, "Get up! Get dressed. Follow me."

The chains fell from Peter's body as he followed the angel right out of the prison and into the dark night.

Peter was free! But he was in danger. If anyone saw him, he would be right back in prison...or worse.

Peter looked for shelter and ran speedily to Mary's house. She was John's mother, and a great many people were gathered at her home praying for Peter.

Peter knocked on the door until a servant girl named Rhoda answered. In her excitement, she slammed the door in Peter's face and ran to tell the group that he was there. But no one believed her.

Peter shouted through the door, "It's me! An angel rescued me from prison. God answered your prayers!"

The people were astounded when Peter told them what happened. The visit was short-lived as Peter had to leave quickly. He feared that Herod's men were close behind.

Peter was right! When Herod discovered Peter's escape, he sent his men everywhere to look for him. They searched all over the city for Peter but could not find him. Herod was so angered by Peter's elusiveness that he even killed his own soldiers when they couldn't find him.

After this, Herod went from Judea to Caesarea. The famine had grown worse, and people did not have much food to eat. Herod happened to be in charge of the food supply, and so when the people heard him speak, they worshipped him, saying, "You have the voice of a god, not man."

Immediately, because he did not praise God, an angel of the Lord struck Herod down, and he was eaten by worms as he took his last breath.

Once again, the church grew as they rejoiced. No earthly king, no matter how strong and mighty, could stop the good news from spreading.

GOOD NEWS SPREADS

ACTS 13

After Peter's narrow escape from Herod, the church at Antioch received some very special news.

The Holy Spirit spoke to the leaders as they were praying one evening, "Send Paul and Barnabas throughout Samaria and to the ends of the earth to tell the world the good news." The church at Antioch prayed for Paul and Barnabas and sent them off.

After a few stops, Paul and Barnabas made their way to a city called Antioch in Pisidia. (This is a different city than the other Antioch.) Both Jews and Gentiles lived there.

The Jews of the city welcomed Paul into the synagogue and asked, "Do you have any words of encouragement for us?"

Paul was delighted by their question and replied, "Fellow children of Abraham (another name for Jews) and you Gentiles who love God, the message of salvation has come to us. You know that God chose you as his people and made you great even when you were slaves in Egypt under evil Pharaoh. He led you out and put up with your grumbling and complaining in the desert for 40 years! He defeated seven nations in the land of Canaan and gave you their land. Your family's travels from Egypt, through the desert, and back to Israel took 450 years. After that, he gave you judges like Samuel the prophet. Then you asked for a king and he gave you Saul for 40 years. God removed him and gave you David, a man after God's heart."

Paul continued, "Through David, God brought you the savior, Jesus. John the Baptist told you about him. This is the good news that saves you! And yet, the rulers in Jerusalem put him to death on a tree and then laid him in a tomb. But he arose three days later and appeared to his disciples."

The people were stunned by what Paul said.

"This Jesus," Paul continued, "is the one who can forgive your sins. He will free you. Some of you look at all the rules and laws, believing that God will love you if you obey. But if you live that way, your hearts will always be hungry. You'll never find the love you long for."

Paul's beautiful words captivated the people because they spoke to the truest parts of who God made them to be.

Everyone wanted to hear more. The next week the entire city gathered to hear Paul speak the word of God. What a glorious scene!

However, the Jewish leaders were not as excited! As the people gathered, their blood boiled with jealousy and they spoke against Paul, "This is absurd! A disgrace! Do not listen to these liars!"

Paul, not one to back down, responded boldly, "The good news is for the Jews first. But you pushed it away. You did not want the eternal life Jesus promises. Now God has asked us to tell the Gentiles the good news. It's as good for them as it is for you."

The Gentiles in the crowd heard these words and rejoiced as they glorified God. Many people believed and received eternal life.

But the Jewish leaders were still outraged. In their anger, they sent big, important men to kick Paul and his friends out of town.

The leaders could remove Paul and Barnabas from their city, but they could not erase what God did in Antioch in Pisidia. Paul and his friends left with smiles on their faces and joy in their hearts because of what the Holy Spirit did through them.

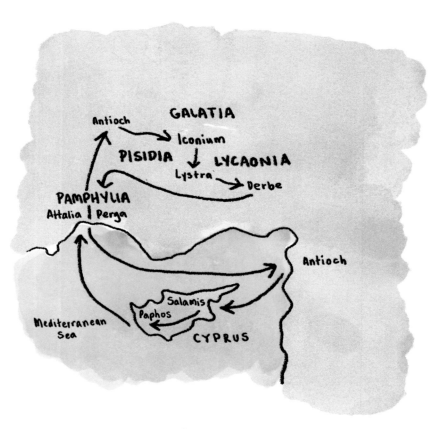

Paul's travels in
Acts 13-14

GOOD NEWS HEALS

ACTS 14

How do you feel when people are mean to you? It can make you feel downright rotten and sad! Our friend, Paul, was no different.

It seemed that everywhere Paul went, people did the most horrible things to him. When he got to a city called Iconium, some people even wanted him dead!

The big, important people of the city mocked Paul, "What's all this 'good news' you're talking about? Not long ago you were killing people for the very things you now want us to believe!"

Most people would keep plenty of distance from anyone who talked to them in that way. But Paul was not like most people. He remembered how Jesus drew near to him when he was full of hate. The good news changed Paul and it made him want to get closer to these men, not farther away!

Paul went to meet with the big, important people. But on his way, he learned that they wanted to hurt him with more than just their words. They wanted to kill him! Wisely, Paul and his friends quickly fled to a nearby city called Lystra.

It became clear right away why God sent Paul to Lystra. One day, as he was teaching a crowd of people, his eyes focused on one man. But this was no ordinary man. His feet did not work. In fact, he had never walked, not even one step in his whole life! Everyone in town pretended like they didn't know him, but God knew him. People thought something was wrong with him, but God was about to make everything right.

Paul looked at the man and proclaimed, "Stand up! Your faith in God has made you well!" Everyone froze. Their eyes were wide with anticipation. Would God do the impossible?

Well, wouldn't you know it! The man stood up. In fact, he sprang up as if he had been walking his whole life. He began trotting around like he'd never missed a beat!

You would have thought the whole town would burst with excitement. Instead, people grew frightened and started wondering if Paul was God.

Of course our friend, Paul would have none of this silliness and instead declared, "I am a man just like you. The God who made heaven and earth has healed him."

But like blind men who could not see, the big, important men could not understand the amazing work of God. Instead, their fear grew into a fierce anger and they made plans to kill Paul.

A mob of men cornered Paul and pummeled him with rocks. Stone after stone struck Paul until everyone thought he was dead. Like cowards, they dragged his bruised and bloodied body outside the city and left him to be eaten by animals.

Paul, though, was not dead. In fact, it was as if God had given him new life! God protected Paul so that the good news of his rescue plan could spread to more and more people.

Paul was back on his feet the very next day, just like the man he healed.

Paul and Barnabas soon left for the city of Derbe. There, they preached the good news, and a large number of people trusted Jesus.

After this, Paul and Barnabas had the courage to go back to Lystra to strengthen the disciples and encourage them to be faithful to Jesus. In Lystra, and in the cities of Iconium, Antioch in Pisidia, Pamphylia, Perga, and Attalia, Paul and Barnabas encouraged the disciples through challenging times. They reminded them of Jesus's own words, "We must go through many hardships to enter the kingdom of God."

Almost everywhere they went, the gospel message brought danger for Paul and his friends. However, new life came to those who had eyes to see and ears to hear the good news.

GOOD NEWS UNITES

ACTS 15

God spread his good news all over the world, but life grew more difficult for the disciples each day.

Men came down from Judea, teaching the disciples they must follow every single law in the Old Testament to be loved by God. But, as we know, that is the exact opposite of the good news!

What we need is not more rule-following. We need Jesus. He obeyed the law perfectly for us and died the death we deserve for our disobedience. When we see how Jesus loved us, we can't help but want to obey him out of love.

Paul and Barnabas were fed up with these lies and went to talk to the church leaders in Jerusalem. Even in Jerusalem, though, Paul and Barnabas found enemies of the good news; men who believed that God will love you if you are just good enough.

However, the real issue was not rule following. Instead, the men were upset about the Gentile Christians! How could God love people who were not Jewish? Leaders from all over came together in Jerusalem for what became known as the Jerusalem Council.

As people gathered, Peter stood and spoke, "Friends and brothers, God asked me to tell the Gentiles the good news. They believed, and God saved them. God knows every man's heart, and he chose to send the Holy Spirit to them. There is no special treatment in God's kingdom. It doesn't matter if you are a Jew or a Gentile. The gospel is for everyone who believes!"

James, who happened to the half-brother of Jesus, agreed. "The prophet Amos, in the Old Testament, promised this would happen. He told us Gentiles would become believers. The Jews do not have a special right to be the only people God loves."

After hearing from Peter and James, all who gathered were united. They agreed that God was doing a great work that should be encouraged and not stopped! Judas and Silas, two well-respected men, were sent to Antioch with a letter for the Gentiles.

"We send you greetings," the letter read. "We have heard of your troubles. People have been violent and mean to you for no good reason. We are sorry. Please know that God loves you, just as he loves the Jews. Jesus himself said that 'his burden is light' and so we want to lay on you no more rules to follow other than these. First, worship God only and not idols made by the hands of men. Second, be married to only one person. God saves you as a gift, but he wants you to follow him with your whole heart. Please do these things we are asking, and you will do well in following him! Farewell."

The Gentile Christians rejoiced at this good news. The weight of years of rejection was lifted from their shoulders. What a wonderful day!

From there, Paul and Barnabas decided to go their separate ways. Barnabas went to Cyprus with another disciple named Mark. Paul took Silas with him to visit the churches he helped start to encourage them and hear about the good work of the Lord.

GOOD NEWS SHAKES THE WORLD

ACTS 16:14-40

Paul and Silas soon made their way to a town called Philippi. It was a very important city with many smart people who thought they had everything figured out. You would think these smart people would be convinced of the good news right away, but they weren't.

That's the thing about believing. It doesn't just happen up in your head. Believing is a work of the Holy Spirit. The truth of God's love has to seep down and change your heart. Because of their unbelief, some people in Philippi opposed the good news and even hated Paul.

One day, Paul and Silas helped a famous person come to know Jesus. Then, they turned around and healed a woman who had an evil spirit living inside her. All of this commotion made the leaders of the city angry!

Philippi's big, important men were sent to beat Paul and Silas and throw them in prison. Could prison bars stop the good news?

What the leaders couldn't see is they were playing right into God's plan to save the world! Nothing, no matter how strong, dark, or scary, could get in the way of God's great plan.

On that first night, Paul and Silas should have been sulking and sad. But they weren't. Just the opposite! They began singing songs of worship to God around midnight. These must have been powerful songs because just then God sent an earthquake! The ground began to shake, the walls began to break, and all the prisoners' chains fell off. The doors flung wide open!

Startled, the prison guard awoke. His heart sank in his chest and his whole body trembled, supposing the prisoners had escaped. In his despair, he drew his sword from his side and readied himself to end his own life.

But, little did he know, his life was not ending. In fact, it was just beginning.

"STOP! We are here!" Paul cried in a loud voice, just in the nick of time.

The guard rushed into the cell and collapsed at Paul and Silas's feet, asking, "What must I do to be saved?"

Paul and Silas shared the good news of Jesus with the guard. They told him about the freedom Jesus's death brings to those who are imprisoned to their sin.

The guard heard all of this and believed because the Holy Spirit gave him ears to hear and eyes to see!

In the wee hours of the morning, he ran home and woke his whole family up. He brought them to Paul to be baptized. They rejoiced because God brought new life from the rubble of an earthquake.

God's great rescue plan often takes very peculiar twists and turns. It is not always the story we would write.

Who would have expected God to put Jonah in the belly of a whale to change his heart? Can you think of one Army general who would have marched around and around Jericho blowing horns to knock the walls down?

But God is unlike anyone. He is the greatest author of all time. He writes his good news into every nook and cranny of history, including an earthquake, in a prison, in the middle of the night.

PAUL THE TRAVELER

ACTS 17-18

From the rubble of an earthquake, Paul and Silas embarked on a whirlwind tour proclaiming the good news to as many people as possible.

Their first stop was Thessalonica. While there, Paul preached in the synagogue for three weeks. He taught the Jews that Jesus had to suffer, die, and be resurrected to give us eternal life. Many Jews, Greeks, and some of the most powerful women around believed and became Christians.

But not everyone was excited. The Jews' jealousy began to boil over. "These men are turning the world upside down!" they shouted as they dragged Paul and Silas before the big, important men of the city. "These men say there's another king besides Caesar and his name is Jesus!" they accused.

Let's pause for a second. Who is this Caesar guy? Why would anyone compare him with King Jesus?

At that time the Caesar was the most important man in the world. He even had a big, long name to prove to everyone just how very important he was: Tiberius Claudius Caesar Augustus Germanicus. What a mouthful! He was in charge of the entire Roman empire and he made all the people worship him like he was a god.

This is why the good news was the best news for the Thessalonians. Jesus was a better, kinder, more powerful king than Caesar. But the Jews couldn't see that Jesus was who their hearts needed most.

It was a tense moment, but the Jews decided to let the disciples go free while taking all their money as punishment.

Next, Paul and Silas set off to tell those living in Berea about Jesus. The Bereans were eager to hear the good news and received it with joy.

Little did Paul and Silas know, however, that the Jews from Thessalonica were following close behind.

Set on destroying any hope the gospel had of taking root, the Thessalonians started a riot in Berea! Quite a violent scene erupted, and Paul and Silas decided it was best to leave so more people could hear the good news.

The Bereans quickly ushered Paul onto a boat while Silas and Timothy, another disciple traveling with them, stayed behind. They hoped to join Paul again soon.

Paul took a quick ride to a nearby city called Athens, where he was out of harm's way. It wasn't long, though, before Paul grew disturbed by what he saw there. Idols, carvings of fake gods, were everywhere!

The leaders of the city grew curious about what Paul believed and invited him to share. "Men of Athens," Paul began, "I can see from all of your idols that you are very religious. One of your idols even says on it 'to the unknown God.'" To the Athenians, God was unknowable. He was far off and wasn't much concerned with people. But Paul knew the one true God was much different.

"God made everything, and he made you. From one man, Adam, he made every nation on the face of the earth. He made us to look for him and find him because he is actually much closer than you think. He wants to know you and be with you," Paul explained.

Some Athenians mocked Paul, but others believed the good news that day and joined him.

From there, Paul took a short journey to the big city of Corinth where he reunited with Silas and Timothy. They were quickly befriended by a Jewish couple, Aquila and his wife Priscilla. This dear family would become Paul's lifelong friends.

Paul lived and worked with Aquila and Priscilla in Corinth for some time. The three of them made tents together as Paul preached in the synagogue every week.

But Aquila and Priscilla were much more than mere tent makers! One time, a very smart man named Apollos came from the city of Alexandria. Apollos thought of Jesus as a great teacher, but did not know he was the savior of the world. Priscilla and Aquila put down their tent-making tools and told Apollos the good news. Apollos's life was changed forever as he continued his travels; only this time with the hope of Jesus!

Priscilla and Aquila help us see that you don't have to be an apostle or a pastor to share the good news. Jesus's call to make disciples is for everyone!

As Paul proclaimed the good news, week after week, the Jews grew violent, and Paul grew more and more frustrated every day.

"I have done all I can. Your blood is on your own hands," Paul reasoned. "The Jews will not listen. From now on, I will only bring the good news to the Gentiles." Discouraged, Paul left the synagogue and walked to the home of a believer named Titius Justus.

There, God comforted Paul and spoke directly to him in a vision, saying, "Don't be afraid, go on speaking to the Jews. I am with you. No one will attack or harm you. I have many people in this city who will believe."

Paul trusted God when he would have rather run away. He stayed in Corinth another eighteen months, teaching the word of God. Just as God said, many came to believe in Jesus. Even the ruler of the synagogue, one of the most committed of the Jews, came to believe the good news!

Eventually, though, some big, important men had enough. They brought charges against Paul in court. Sensing that only danger lay ahead of him in Corinth, Paul left and began the long journey back home.

Paul made several stops on his way back to Antioch. Taking Priscilla and Aquila with him, he went to Ephesus to talk with the Jews and to Caesarea to visit friends.

All told, these travels took more than three years. Can you imagine leaving home and not returning for over 1,000 days? When he arrived back home in Antioch, Paul had lots to tell his friends. For the next two years, Paul traveled from church to church, strengthening them and sharing what God did through his travels.

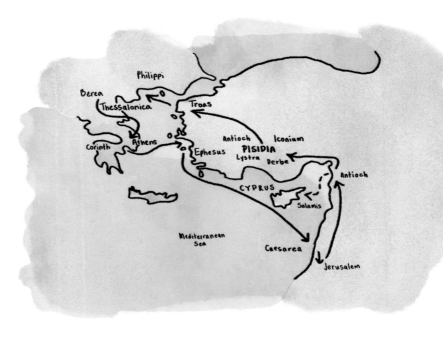

Paul's travels in Acts 15-18

GOOD NEWS STARTS A RIOT

ACTS 19

After two years at home, Paul set out on the road again to tell more people the good news. He eventually made his way back to Ephesus, which was one of his final stops on his last journey. It must have been wonderful to see these good friends after several years!

Paul picked up right where he left off in Ephesus and began sharing the good news. What people heard changed their lives.

As God spoke through Paul, incredible things began happening all around. Many people believed and were baptized. A group of men were so excited about the good news that they got together to preach about the kingdom of God and didn't stop for three months!

After Paul was in Ephesus for two years, everyone for miles around had heard the good news of God's great rescue!

It was almost too good to be true. Paul finally found a place where the gospel took root and was spreading quickly. Could the good times last?

They didn't! Before long, there was a new group of big, important people who didn't like what Paul was doing one little bit. They had big, important jobs making and selling art. But this was no ordinary art. They sold sculptures of a make-believe god named Artemis.

Many people in Ephesus worshipped Artemis instead of the one true God. When the townspeople heard the good news of Jesus, though, they realized all of this was silly and stopped buying sculptures of Artemis. This sent the artists into quite the tizzy!

"Where is he?!" One of the artists, named Demetrius, finally had enough! "Who does Paul think he is? He thinks he can just march in here and tell us how to live?" Demetrius questioned.

Demetrius's face was red with anger. He called all the people of Ephesus to the center of town and started a big, huge riot. There was lots of pushing and shoving, yelling and carrying on with all sorts of ridiculous nonsense. What a crazy scene!

Many of Paul's closest friends were dragged away by the crowds, beaten, and made fun of. People shouted, "Great is Artemis! Great is Artemis! Great is Artemis!" at the top of their lungs. The madness went on for hours upon hours until a wise town leader calmed them all down.

"These men have done nothing wrong. There is no good reason for you to make a scene like this. Let these men go free unless you want to bring charges against them in a court of law," the leader reasoned.

Seeing that their rioting was foolish, the crowd quickly scattered and went back to their homes.

Demetrius was shocked. He simply couldn't stop the good news. It was just that good! God was at work showing this city (and us!) that it's silly to love anything more than God.

The people of Ephesus were foolish to worship their statues of Artemis. Today, we can still love lots of things more than God. It might be sports, fame, money, success, or even our friends. God wants us to know that he made us to love him above everything else. Demetrius thought that money and popularity would make him happy. But in the end, it only made him miserable.

God knew there were still many more people who needed to hear this good news. People like you and me! His rescue plan was spreading to all the people of the earth and nothing would stop him.

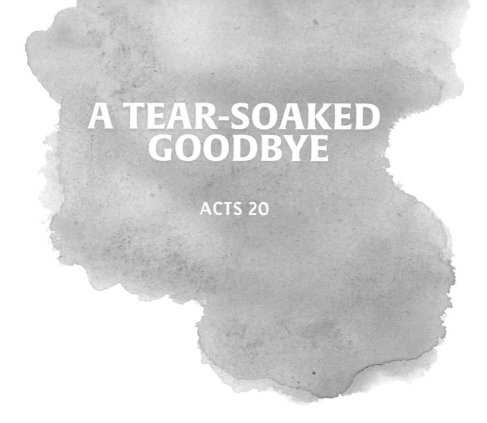

A TEAR-SOAKED GOODBYE

ACTS 20

After the riot, Paul and his friends were on the move visiting towns around Ephesus. By boat or by land, it seemed the disciples were always finding new places to share the good news.

One night, in the town of Troas, Paul was teaching a group of men long after dark. As you can imagine, people grew quite sleepy. A young boy, named Eutyches, even fell asleep while Paul was speaking. Perhaps it was past his bedtime! Before anyone could holler, "Wake up!" he fell right out of a third-story window!

Everyone thought Eutyches was dead. But Paul, with just a word, announced that he was alive.

Extraordinary things like this seemed to happen all the time. The Holy Spirit was at work, showing the power of God everywhere the disciples went.

After traveling to many cities, Paul journeyed back to Ephesus. Paul had a soft spot for the people of Ephesus. He loved the city and the church. But Paul was nervous because he had sad news to share.

"You know that I love you very much," Paul began as he spoke to the elders. "When I was with you, I told the Jews and the Gentiles the good news of Jesus. We saw people repent and turn to God."

The elders nodded in agreement, thankful for what God had done through their friendship.

Paul continued, "But now I must go to Jerusalem."

Jerusalem?! The elder's faces quickly fell from happiness to horror.

"The Holy Spirit told me to go, and I must obey. I know what awaits me there. I will be arrested and probably killed because I have shared the good news with you and the rest of the world," Paul explained.

The Ephesian Christians were filled with sorrow. Sobs shook their bodies. Could this be the last time they would see their friend? Could a man God used so mightily really be put to death? To some, it must have seemed that he was following in the steps of another man. Jesus went to Jerusalem, did nothing wrong, and was put to death to bring life to the world.

"God has put it on my heart to do this, and I must obey. I must finish the work he has for me," Paul reasoned. "God gave me life when my heart was dead. If he would receive glory in my death, then I consider losing my life an honor."

The elders were deeply moved by Paul's words. They gathered around, got down on their knees, and prayed for him.

They wept...a lot. They hugged...a lot.

Then the elders walked Paul to his ship and watched as he set sail. They must have walked slowly, soaking up every last moment. When God forms friendships like these, the goodbyes are gut-wrenching.

"Farewell, Paul. Until we meet again," they said, almost all cried out of tears.

When we follow Jesus, our lives belong to him. He is the one who rescues us from death and gives us eternal life. In a way, then, he owns our lives. Sometimes he may call us to do brave, courageous things. Maybe he will even ask us to do dangerous things.

But, like Paul, we can trust God no matter what he asks of us. He has planned all of our steps and, if we have trusted Jesus, has given us eternal life with him.

Paul's travels in Acts 19-21

BACK IN JERUSALEM

ACTS 21-22

Paul and his friends set sail for Jerusalem, but they were a long way from home. In fact, they were almost 600 miles away! Since the travels were quite long, they made several visits along the way.

In each place, people urged Paul to stop what he was doing. Just like the Ephesian elders, everyone knew if Paul went back to Jerusalem, he would be put to death!

"Are you out of your mind?" asked a man named Agabus in Caesarea.

Agabus took Paul's belt off his waist, wrapped it around his hands and feet, and got up in his face, "Don't you know this is what they will do to you in Jerusalem? I tell you now, you must stop!"

"Why are you doing this?" Paul asked. "This is already hard enough, but I am ready to die for Jesus if that is his plan."

Agabus released Paul and, with tears welling up in his eyes, said farewell.

Eventually, Paul arrived in Jerusalem. He met with James and the elders of the church right away. Together, the men rejoiced as they heard about God's work among the Gentiles.

However, it was a nervous type of celebration.

"The Gospel we love, and you have been teaching, is about Jesus. He has fulfilled the law. That means there is nothing anyone needs to do to be loved by God. We only need to receive the gift of Jesus. But there are Jews who still think people need to follow the hundreds and hundreds of Old Testament laws to make God love them," the elders explained.

As we have seen before in Acts, there are lots of laws in the Old Testament. There are laws about cleaning your dishes and where to sleep, and even how to grow your hair.

But God never gave hundreds of laws to show us how to earn his love. Instead, they show us that we can't make him love us because following all the laws was never the point. The law is supposed to point us away from ourselves and to our need of Jesus. He chooses to care for us. His love is a free gift. The Jews in Jerusalem, however, did not understand this.

Paul and the elders discussed all of this and agreed, "To win the trust of the Jews and to honor what Jesus has done, we need to show that we respect the law. After all, God gave it to us. There is nothing wrong with showing that we hold the law in high regard, even if we don't believe following it earns you anything."

As Paul lived among the Jews, he even agreed to go seven days without eating grapes and raisins and to not cut his hair. At the end of the seven days, he would shave his head bald. This, of course, was one of the hundreds and hundreds of laws.

When the seven days were almost finished, the Jews saw Paul in the temple.

"There he is!" The crowd erupted with shouting and screaming.

The big, important men grabbed Paul, bound him with chains, and took him away.

Paul was inches away from being thrown in jail when he pleaded, "I am a man just like you. Please, let me speak to the people."

The guards stopped. Paul stood up and motioned to the crowd with his hand. A great hush fell over the people.

Paul began, "I am just like you, a Jew by birth. I went to school with the best teachers and learned all about God. I love the law, but I put it above God's love for me. It made me hate others. I killed many people, and I would have killed even more if God didn't stop me. I was on the road to Damascus when he made my eyes blind so I would see the blindness of my heart. In his kindness, he sent a man named Ananias to explain the good news to me. It changed my life."

What an incredible moment! What a reflection of what God had done for him! Beautiful words spilled from Paul's lips as he loved those who only wished him harm.

Paul continued, "I came back to Jerusalem, but I could not stay. I was guilty. There was blood on my hands from the murder of Stephen. God told me to leave and go preach the good news to the Gentiles."

"You just stop right there!" The big, important men did not like any talk of the Gentiles. They raised their voices. "Away with you, kill him!"

In a split second, the men stretched Paul out on a wooden board. They reared back with whips in hand, ready to end Paul's life. Just then, Paul remembered that he had a way to get the men to stop.

Years before, the Romans invaded Jerusalem. The city and all the surrounding areas were now controlled by the Roman empire. Paul, by birth, happened to be a citizen of Rome.

Paul looked up and quickly explained, "You can't kill me. I am a Roman citizen and we are on Roman soil. You must give me a fair trial and let me plead my case."

By the skin of his teeth, Paul had dodged death once again. Paul would get his day in court. In fact, he would not have to wait very long at all.

PAUL'S DAY IN COURT

ACTS 23

The room was cold with nervous anticipation. What would happen? Jesus was not given a fair trial. Would Paul, a follower of Jesus, get one?

The guards unlocked Paul's chains before he spoke, "Brothers, I have lived my life before God with a clear mind and heart."

WHACK!

Ananias, the high priest of the Jews, commanded the soldiers to hit Paul right across the mouth.

Immediately Paul shook off the blow. "That was nothing compared to how God is going to strike you for your evil ways. You pretend to love God, but you hate people. You try to hide your evil with rule-following, but God sees you," Paul insisted.

God had prepared Paul with confidence for just a time like this. Paul wisely looked around, noticing that on one half of the room sat the Pharisees. They were zealous for the law but did not believe Jesus freed us from it as a way of earning God's love. Curiously, though, they did believe that people could be resurrected from the dead.

On the other half of the room were the Sadducees. They didn't believe that Jesus was resurrected from the dead.

Seeing this, Paul quickly devised a clever plan. "Brothers, as you know, I am one of you," Paul said as he motioned to the Pharisees. Paul then turned and looked right at the Sadducees, saying, "What we are here to do today is in regard to the hope we have because Jesus was resurrected."

What a smart move by Paul. Now the two sides of the room were more upset with one another over their disagreement than they were with Paul! In an instant, the court grew violent as a great clamor arose. To save themselves from getting hurt, the Pharisees quickly moved to halt the proceedings, "There is nothing wrong with Paul, we dismiss our case!"

What an amazing day! But, if you thought the story was over, you'd be wrong.

The next morning, the Jews plotted together and devised a sinister plan to kill Paul. Forty men agreed to not eat or drink until he was dead. Grumbling stomachs can be quite a good motivator!

"Let's tell Paul to come back to court," the forty men sneakily suggested to Ananias, "and when he gets close, before he goes in the building, we will kill him."

What they didn't know, though, was that Paul's nephew had been spying on them the whole time. He heard everything and ran as fast he could to warn his uncle before it was too late.

Once Paul heard the plan, he asked the soldiers to bring his nephew to the courthouse. Paul's nephew told the court everything he knew, and the case was quickly dismissed.

God knows what is inside every human heart. He knows our secrets and our selfish thoughts. It's a good thing he does! On this day God knew the plan to kill Paul and he saved his life. But would Paul ever get a fair trial?

FELIX AND FESTUS

ACTS 24-26

It became clearer by the day that Paul would never be treated fairly in Jerusalem. At every turn in the road, people did the nastiest and most violent things to him. Paul knew it was time to use his special status as a Roman citizen once again in order to save his life.

"Bring me to Caesarea at once," Paul demanded. "I am a Roman citizen and deserve to have my case heard by Felix, the governor of Judea."

For safety, Paul traveled the 55 miles north to Caesarea in the middle of the night, on horseback, with nearly 500 guards!

Upon learning that Paul was, in fact, a Roman, Felix agreed to a trial. He called for Ananias, the high priest, and his spokesman, Tertullus, to come to Caesarea at once.

Upon arriving, Tertullus gushed with praise, "We love you, Felix. Thank you for all the kind things you have done for our land. You are an excellent and wonderful man." He was buttering up Felix, hoping to get him on his side.

Tertullus continued, "We love our nation so much that we cannot stand by while this plague of a man lives here."

Paul? A plague?

Felix looked at Paul, "Are these things true?"

Paul answered, "My mind and heart are clear before God.
These men are lying to you. I only want to do what God
has asked of me: to tell the world that Jesus has come to
give us eternal life."

Felix ordered Paul back to prison, but instructed the guards to be kind to him.

Of course, we would like to believe that Felix was being nice because he was a decent person. However, all along he hoped that one of Paul's friends would give him a pile of money as a bribe to get Paul out of prison.

However, this never happened. Paul was an honest man and God had a plan for him during his two years in prison.

One day, Felix brought his wife, Drusilla, down to meet Paul. She was Jewish, and so she was curious as to what this prisoner had to share.

One of the most powerful men in all the world brought the woman he loved most to Paul! Would he tell her the good news, even though it meant risking his own life?

Absolutely! Paul boldly shared with Drusilla about righteousness, self-control, and the coming judgment for her if she did not believe in Jesus. Felix was alarmed to say the least. He had never seen someone stand up to him like this! Paul respected Felix, but he served Jesus.

Later on, Felix was removed from office and replaced by a new governor named Festus.

Things would get better under this new leader, right? Sad news...they did not.

After only three days, Festus went to Jerusalem where the Jewish leaders laid out their case against Paul. The leaders urged Festus to bring Paul back to Jerusalem so they could hide along the roadside and kill him on his way.

Seeing their plan, Festus answered, "Why don't you bring your people here, to Caesarea? If you can prove there is something wrong with Paul, I will bring him to Jerusalem."

Ten days later, the Jewish leaders were with Festus and Paul in Caesarea bringing all sorts of unprovable, ridiculous charges.

"This is simply not true!" Paul pleaded.

But Festus's heart had grown dark and he asked the Jews if they wanted to have a trial in Jerusalem. What was he thinking?! Of course they did!

"Stop right there!" Paul insisted. "If you think I have done something wrong, then just kill me now. But I want to go to the highest court. I appeal to Caesar, and I want to see Agrippa, the king. I have that right as a Roman citizen."

Festus was forced to agree with Paul.

Some days later, King Agrippa arrived with his sister, Bernice, in Caesarea.

"This man, Paul, has been a prisoner for some time," Festus explained as he caught the leader up to speed. "I have heard his side and the Jews' side of the story and my opinion is that he has not broken the law but that they are simply having a dispute over religion."

Were the tables turning? Was Festus now on Paul's side?

With great fanfare and flourish, in a fancy room decked out for the king, Paul met with Agrippa the following day.

Festus gave a defense of Paul. He explained that, while he disagreed with Paul, there was no reason to keep him in prison. Agrippa then motioned for Paul to speak.

Paul began, "I am a prisoner on earth because I am free in God's eyes. I have the hope of eternal life. Jesus has come and rescued me. I once hated him, but he changed my heart with his great love for me. God promised Moses that Jesus would come, and he has. He has come to set free those who are captive to their sin."

The whole room stood still with nervous anticipation. How would the king respond?

Agrippa looked Paul right in the eyes and asked the most surprising question, "How can I be a Christian?"

The Pharisees and Sadducees tried to kill him, Felix tried to chain him up for life, but God wanted Paul here for this moment. One of the most important men in the world heard the good news that day.

Festus concluded, "This man should be free for he has done nothing wrong."

ON TO ROME

Paul was on his way to freedom. However, one more hurdle lay before him. In the course of his time in court, Paul had appealed to Caesar. This meant he would need to appear before the court in Rome. The Roman empire was huge at this time, and the capitol was 1,400 miles away from Caesarea. That is one long trip!

Some days later, Paul boarded a big cargo ship and set sail while it made many deliveries throughout the Roman Empire.

It wasn't long before Paul and the crew saw the weather growing worse. Powerful storms shook the boat. Paul urged the crew to use caution, but they would not listen. The boat was tossed to and fro and eventually shipwrecked on an island called Malta.

How could our friend be rescued? Nobody had ever heard of a cell phone or a rescue helicopter in Paul's time. Paul and his companions were stuck!

But God had a plan to take care of them.

As it turned out, the people on the island were unusually kind. It was as if God had made them ready to receive their new guests. How refreshing this must have been for Paul after years of mistreatment!

One day, the weather on the island was unusually cold. To keep warm, Paul built a fire. He was gathering up twigs, sticks, and firewood when...SNAP! A viper jumped out, sunk his teeth into Paul's hand, and would not let go!

"Look, justice cannot be escaped. Paul is a murderer, and it has caught up to him!" the people of the island mocked, knowing Paul was a prisoner.

But God was not done protecting Paul. He simply flicked his wrist and shook the snake off into the fire. Everyone looked with dread at Paul, knowing in mere seconds he would certainly swell up or fall dead. But neither of those things happened. It was as if nothing happened at all!

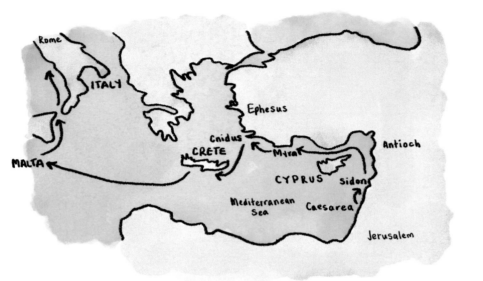

Paul's travels in Acts 27-28

Paul lived on the island for three months. He healed people of their diseases and told them the good news. In hindsight, this must have been an encouraging time for Paul. He was around people who loved him and wished him no harm.

After some time, a ship on its way to Rome stopped by the island. Paul got on board and set sail again.

In Rome, Paul met with the Roman officials. Great numbers of people came to hear Paul as his fame spread far and wide.

From morning until night, the Romans heard the good news. Many were convinced, but some were not and eventually dismissed Paul to live amongst them.

• •

The Book of Acts ends right there. It is an abrupt ending to a wonderful book. But it is not the end of the story. We know from other books in the Bible that Paul's ministry continued.

Jesus told his disciples to spread the good news in Jerusalem, Judea, Samaria, and to the ends of the earth. You are reading these words today because people like Peter, Stephen, Paul, Cornelius, Barnabas, Silas, Festus, Agrippa, and so many others heard Jesus's command and obeyed.

Together, let's continue their legacy with our families and friends because we believe that God is not done yet. Just as God reminded Paul in Corinth, there are still many more who need to hear the life-giving words of Jesus.